The Army in Action

Susan Sawyer
AR B.L.: 10.3
Points: 3.0   UG

THE ARMY IN ACTION

U.S. Military Branches and Careers

THE ARMY IN ACTION

Susan Sawyer

Enslow Publishers, Inc.
40 Industrial Road   PO Box 38
Box 398   Aldershot
Berkeley Heights, NJ 07922 Hants GU12 6BP
USA   UK

http://www.enslow.com

Library of Congress Cataloging-in-Publication Data

Sawyer, Susan.
    The Army in action / Susan Sawyer.
       p. cm. — (U.S. military branches and careers)
    Includes bibliographical references and index.
    ISBN 0-7660-1635-8 (library binding)
    1. United States. Army—Vocational guidance—Juvenile literature.
[1. United States. Army—Vocational guidance. 2. Vocational
guidance.]   I. Title. II. Series.
UA23 .S293 2001
355'.0023'73—dc21

                                    2001000194

Printed in the United States of America

10 9 8 7 6 5 4

To Our Readers: We have done our best to make sure all Internet addresses in
this book were active and appropriate when we went to press. However, the
author and the publisher have no control over and assume no liability for the
material available on those Internet sites or on other Web sites they may link to.
Any comments or suggestions can be sent by e-mail to comments@enslow.com or
to the address on the back cover.

Illustration Credits: All photos are courtesy U.S. Department of
Defense, except for the following: National Archives, pp. 17, 19, 21, 22,
24, 26, 28, 29, 30, 31, 33, 34, 35, 36, 38, 44, 73, 88, 89, 90, 91, 97,
98, 100; U.S. Army, p. 114.

Cover Illustrations: U.S. Department of Defense.

Contents

The Mission and Role of Today's Soldiers

Frigid winds blasted through the morning air as United States Army soldiers gathered at the edge of a field in Bosnia. Preparing to launch a dangerous mission, the soldiers from the 754th Ordnance Company quickly set up the equipment and machines they needed.

Trained as explosive disposal specialists, the soldiers knew exactly what they had to do. According to reports from local residents, a young child had spotted something that looked like an unexploded bomb in the frozen field. Now the soldiers were faced with the task of finding and dismantling it before it could explode.

Within a few minutes, two soldiers dressed in protective body armor walked onto the field. Each man carried a device for detecting metal objects. Resembling a trimmer for edging lawns, the device would emit a sound when it found metal in the field.

The men proceeded with caution, well aware that they could trip over a hidden land mine at any minute and be blown to pieces. Other members of their unit stood in silence at the edge of the field, watching.

Proceeding with caution, this soldier uses a mine detector to search the ground for any unexploded mines.

Suddenly a sound erupted from one of the detectors. The two men carefully placed a marker on the spot and retreated cautiously from the field. The rest of the soldiers prepared for action, ready to uncover the object.

After locating and identifying the object as an unexploded bomb, the soldiers removed the explosive from the field. Then they defused it. By the end of the morning, the soldiers had successfully accomplished their mission.

Ready for their next task of the day, the soldiers prepared to go to a local school. During the afternoon, they would teach Bosnian schoolchildren how to recognize and identify dangerous explosives. Like the unexploded bomb in the Bosnian field, many explosive devices from the country's civil war remain scattered throughout villages and towns. By some estimates, more than 5 million land mines were planted in Bosnia. If not properly recovered and defused, the explosives could harm or kill innocent people.[1]

The soldiers of the United States Army are part of an international peacekeeping mission in Bosnia. The country is located in southeastern Europe and is about the same size as the state of West Virginia. Its official name is Bosnia and Herzegovina.

In 1992, Bosnia and Herzegovina was established as a republic in the former country of Yugoslavia. For the next three years, three Bosnian groups—Muslims, Croats, and Serbs—turned the republic into a battlefield. More than two hundred thousand people were killed and thousands of people lost their homes during the Bosnian civil war.[2]

In 1995 the heads of the three warring parties traveled to the United States and signed a peace

Two U.S. Army soldiers take time to explain to these Bosnian children about the dangers of mines and to hand out some NBA basketball cards.

agreement in Dayton, Ohio. The agreement, known as the Dayton Accord, ended the bloody war. To make sure that all parties honored the terms of the agreement, the North Atlantic Treaty Organization (NATO) sent an international peacekeeping force to Bosnia.

During 1995 and 1996, the United States provided twenty thousand troops for the mission. As the armed forces of the NATO countries worked together, maintaining peace and gradually restoring order to the country, NATO was able to reduce the size of the peacekeeping force.[3]

By 2000 there were about four thousand members of the United States Army stationed in Bosnia. Like the soldiers from the 754th Ordnance Company, these troops are making sure that the Bosnian people continue to enjoy peaceful times in their country.[4]

Finding and dismantling explosives is only one of the many tasks performed by U.S. soldiers in Bosnia. Hundreds of soldiers operate equipment and repair machinery. Army doctors perform emergency surgery, aviators fly helicopter missions, and tankers drive Army tanks. Civil affairs officers work with the Bosnian people and government officials, while military police patrol the streets of the war-torn country.

Other soldiers cook food, keep records, and fuel vehicles in Army camps that have been set up throughout the country. Thousands of miles away from home, the soldiers live, eat, work, and sleep in the Army's compounds. During their leisure time, troops take

The Army sends troops to many places around the world to restore peace or help out in a time of crisis.

advantage of the camp's food court, exercise facility, movie tent, cappuccino bar, and chapel. But they stand guard around the clock, making sure they accomplish their mission in Bosnia.[5]

As U.S. soldiers continue to restore peace in Bosnia, thousands of Army troops are working in other places around the globe. These soldiers protect America's worldwide interests, maintain stability in war-torn regions such as Bosnia, and promote peace and prosperity throughout the world.[6]

The Army also sends additional troops to many countries to provide assistance during times of military crisis, civil disturbance, and national disaster. On any given day, an average of 29,000 active duty, National Guard, and Army Reserve soldiers are serving the nation in as many as 122 countries.[7]

About 360,000 Army soldiers are stationed at posts throughout the United States, ready to respond to calls for assistance at home or in foreign countries.[8] They receive training and instruction to gain technical skills and in-depth knowledge about weapons and tactics. They also provide disaster relief to dozens of America's cities and towns every year, fighting such hazardous conditions as floods, wildfires, and hurricanes.

Mission and Role of the U.S. Army

The primary mission of the United States Army, however, is to support and defend the Constitution of the United States. It does this by preserving the peace and security of the country and defending it in times of war or insurrection. The Army is also charged with the responsibility of protecting any trust territories or commonwealths associated with the United States, such as Puerto Rico and Guam.

The Army's mission includes the tasks of supporting U.S. policies, implementing national objectives, and overcoming any nation responsible for aggressive acts that threaten the peace and security of the United States.

To accomplish these missions, the United States Army organizes, trains, and equips forces that can wage combat on land. The Army also supplies combat troops with support services ranging from transportation to health care. Ready to respond to any crisis,

U.S. Army engineers work to complete a pontoon bridge that will link Croatia to Bosnia and Herzegovina.

America's Army is prepared and equipped to defend the nation and preserve peace at all times.

Congress appropriates money to fund the operations of the United States Army each year. The Army's annual budget for 2001 was more than $73.7 billion.[9] Pay and incentives for soldiers make up the largest part of this budget. Another large portion goes toward the development of highly technical equipment, such as sophisticated weapons and advanced communications devices.

With the most modern equipment in the world, today's Army depends on soldiers who can adapt to the demands of technology. To attract the best and

Soldiers in the Army can receive specialized training in such areas as helicopter repair and maintenance.

brightest young people into its ranks, the Army offers many incentives for joining, such as financial assistance for educational costs, enlistment bonuses, and training opportunities. Soldiers can receive training in over two hundred specialties that range from positions in combat areas to public affairs. Every year more than 180,000 young men and women graduate from the Army's 18 major technical training complexes.[10]

From the fields of Bosnia to the Army's headquarters in the Pentagon, American soldiers are committed to duty, honor, and country. As the most powerful military organization in the world, the United States Army depends on its soldiers to protect and defend the nation's interests at home and around the globe.

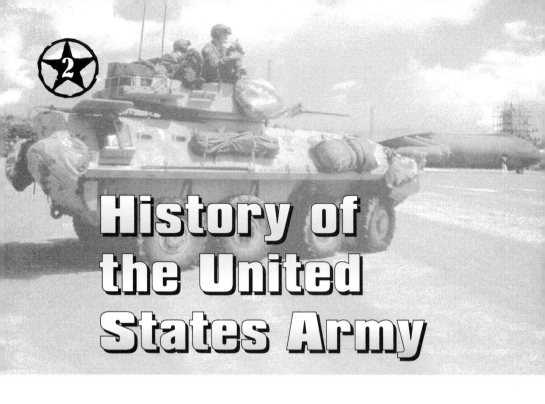

History of the United States Army

Before the United States was formed in 1776, ordinary citizens in the American colonies banded together to defend their families and homes. These small military groups, known as militias, were the forerunners of the United States Army. Each of the thirteen colonies formed militias to provide protection for their colonists.

Unlike the Army of the twenty-first century, colonial militiamen were not professionally trained soldiers. Most were farmers or shopkeepers who wore homespun clothing and used their own weapons for fighting.[1] They shared a love for their new country and the determination to protect their homes and possessions.

The British government, however, did not like the independent ways of the American colonists.

Beginning in 1763, British leaders wanted stricter control of their colonies. In England, Parliament passed new laws and taxes for the American colonies. The colonists had no voice in Parliament, and many Americans resented these laws and taxes. They said it was "taxation without representation."

To make sure that the colonists obeyed the British laws, the English king, George III, stationed British troops throughout the American colonies. The colonists resented the presence of the British "redcoats," and they disliked being taxed by faraway England.

As tensions increased, the Massachusetts militia exchanged gunfire with the redcoats on April 19, 1775, at Lexington, Massachusetts, and at nearby

The Battle of Lexington, fought between the Massachusetts militia and the British Army, was the first battle of the Revolutionary War.

Concord. The battles of Lexington and Concord marked the beginning of the Revolutionary War.

The Revolutionary War

Although the Americans forced the British to retreat at Lexington, the colonists realized they needed more troops to fight against the British. Soon other colonies joined forces with the Massachusetts militia to form the New England Army.

The birthday of the United States Army occurred on June 14, 1775, when the Second Continental Congress voted to adopt the New England militia as the nation's official army. At the same time, Congress voted to enlist the additional services of ten companies of riflemen from Pennsylvania, Maryland, and Virginia. These combined groups formed the Continental Army, the nation's first armed forces, which would later be known as the United States Army.

Congress appointed a Virginia planter, George Washington, commander in chief of the Continental Army. Congress also established the Board of War and Ordnance to oversee the Army's supplies. Supplying the Continental Army with manpower became the responsibility of the states.

The states' recruiting efforts fell short of General Washington's hope for twenty thousand troops. Since soldiers volunteered to serve in the Army for one year, they usually returned home to their families after completing their military obligations. Lacking fresh replacements for the departing soldiers, the Continental Army rarely operated with more than fifteen thousand troops.[2]

Along with insufficient manpower, the Continental soldiers faced shortages of food and supplies. By contrast, the redcoats were well supplied and were well trained. Many were long-term, professional soldiers

George Washington
(1732–1799)

General George Washington served as the first commander in chief of the Continental Army when it was formed in 1775. He held the new army together and defeated the British during the Revolutionary War. Following his successful military career, he became the first president of the United States.

with years of experience. How could America's untrained citizen-soldiers defeat the British, the most powerful military force in the world?

Despite the obstacles encountered by the Continental Army, Washington held his troops together throughout the war. He organized the Army into three divisions: infantry units, with soldiers who fought battles on foot; artillery troops, armed with cannons and other large guns; and cavalry units, with soldiers who rode on horses. Working together, the troops discovered they were better at fighting in the hills and woods than the redcoats, who had been trained to fight battles in open fields.

France and other countries came to the aid of the Continental Army, providing troops, supplies, and money for the American cause. Backed by strong allies and the determination to gain independence from England, Washington and his volunteer army won the Revolutionary War in 1783.

During the war, Congress replaced the Board of War and Ordnance with a civilian leader, the secretary at war, who reported directly to Congress. With the adoption of the United States Constitution in 1789, Congress established a new organizational structure for the Army and created the Department of War. The new president, George Washington, became commander in chief of the Army and Navy, and the title "secretary at war" was changed to "secretary of war." As head of the department, the secretary of war reported directly to the president instead of Congress.

After the Revolution

Congress realized that America needed to maintain troops for the defense and protection of the new nation. Under the Militia Act of 1792, Congress provided that every male citizen was obliged to defend his nation. Washington and other military leaders recommended the establishment of a special school for training and educating future soldiers. Following Washington's advice, Congress approved the creation of the United States Military Academy at West Point, New York, in 1802.

After the Militia Act of 1792, posters trying to attract new recruits were quite common.

Andrew Jackson
(1767–1845)

Major General Andrew Jackson led army troops to a victory over the Creek Indians in 1814. The following year he gained national fame for defeating the British in the Battle of New Orleans. In 1828 he was elected to serve as the seventh president of the United States.

GEN. ANDREW JACKSON.
THE HERO OF NEW ORLEANS

After James Madison became president of the United States, Congress worked to improve the organization of the Army. They divided the Army into two parts: a general staff, located in Washington, D.C., which provided military leadership, and line units with infantry, artillery, and cavalry soldiers stationed at Army posts throughout the country.

As the United States focused on the organization of its troops, the British stirred up trouble for Americans on the high seas. After the British seized several American ships and held the sailors as prisoners, Congress declared war on England in June 1812. Congress also voted to increase the size of the Army from 6,000 to 25,000 men and authorized the president to call 30,000 militiamen into service.[3]

During the War of 1812, America triumphed in many battles at sea. Although most of the Army's land battles were not successful, Americans applauded General Andrew Jackson's victory over the British during the Battle of New Orleans. The battle came after a peace treaty had been signed in Ghent, Belgium, in 1814, but before news of the treaty reached America.

For the next thirty years, the Army focused on protecting the American frontier. Army troops headed west, fighting Indians, surveying land, and building roads. They also developed new methods of transportation by water, using flat-bottomed boats and pontoon wagons lined with rubber cloth for carrying men and supplies across rivers.

The Mexican War

Once part of Mexico, Texas operated as an independent nation after General Sam Houston defeated General Santa Anna of Mexico in a battle in 1836. To regain control over the territory, Mexicans began attacking Texas settlers. After annexing Texas as a state in 1845, the United States went to the defense of Texas residents, leading to war with Mexico in 1846.

During the Mexican War, United States Army troops applied their new skills in water transportation and used new methods of fighting. Instead of riding into battle on gun carriages that hauled huge cannons, soldiers charged into battle more quickly by riding on horseback. These "flying artillery" units became

After Texas was made a state in 1845, war broke out between the United States and Mexico. Shown is the Battle of Molina del Rey in 1847.

famous. With the success of their new tactics, the United States Army won the Mexican War in less than two years.[4]

After the end of the Mexican War in 1848, Army troops explored the new state of Texas and located routes for transcontinental railroads throughout the western frontier.

When Jefferson Davis became secretary of war in 1853, he established new cavalry regiments for the frontier. He also provided new weapons for the cavalry units, replacing muzzle-loading muskets with breech-loading rifles.

The Civil War

As the United States continued its westward expansion, tensions mounted over the issue of extending slavery into the western territories. One month after Abraham Lincoln's election to the presidency in 1860, South Carolina withdrew from the Union in disagreement over the slavery issue. Ten other southern states soon joined forces with South Carolina. These states—Alabama, Arkansas, Florida, Georgia, Louisiana, Mississippi, North Carolina, South Carolina, Tennessee, Texas, and Virginia—established the Confederate States of America. The new Confederacy chose Jefferson Davis, the former secretary of war, to serve as president.

Union and Confederate troops exchanged gunfire for the first time at Fort Sumter, South Carolina, on April 12, 1861, plunging the nation into civil war. Because the Union lacked enough volunteers and state militiamen to serve as soldiers, Congress passed the Enrollment Act of 1863, the government's first draft law. Under the new law, the Union raised one million troops during the course of the war, while the southern states raised around six hundred thousand soldiers.[5] Infantry (ground) troops accounted for the majority of the forces.

Both sides took advantage of new developments during the Civil War. Improved weapons provided greater accuracy. Telegraph lines enabled commanders in the field to keep in touch with other Army leaders fighting elsewhere. New techniques for waging war included using river gunboats, observation balloons, and ironclad warships.

The telegraph was an important new method of communication during the Civil War. This soldier is cutting the telegraph wires and reconnecting the ends to make it difficult to find where the line was broken.

Throughout four years of fighting, both the Union and the Confederate armies suffered heavy losses. More than 623,000 Union and Confederate soldiers were killed in battle or died in prison from disease or injuries.[6]

The bloody Civil War officially ended on April 9, 1865, when Confederate general Robert E. Lee surrendered to Union general Ulysses S. Grant at Appomattox Courthouse in Virginia. After the war the Army helped to rebuild the southern states. During the Reconstruction period, Army troops occupied the South and provided a form of military government in many southern towns.

Following the Civil War, the Army returned to the western frontier and paved the way for new settlers. Army troops often clashed with Indian tribes who resented the presence of white men on their lands. With the help of new machine guns known as Gatling guns, the United States Army gained control over Indian territories and conquered the western frontier. In 1890 the Army's final victory over warring Indian tribes took place at Wounded Knee, South Dakota.

The Spanish-American War

At the end of the nineteenth century, Americans focused their attention on problems in Cuba, a colony of Spain in the Caribbean. The United States supported the Cubans in a revolt against Spain. In February 1898, the United States battleship *Maine* mysteriously exploded in the harbor of Havana, Cuba. In April, the

Ulysses S. Grant
(1822–1885)

General Ulysses S. Grant served as the commander of the Union Army during the Civil War. Grant led the Union Army to victory and accepted the surrender of Confederate general Robert E. Lee in 1865. After the war, Grant served as president of the United States from 1869 to 1877.

U.S. Congress declared war on Spain. The United States later discovered that the ship's explosion had been caused by defective parts and not by aggressive actions on the part of Spain.

Between the regular Army and volunteer units, a total of 275,000 Army troops served in the Spanish-American War. Although the Navy fought most of the battles in the war, troops from the regular Army and volunteer units participated in many important battles on land. The United States won the war and helped Cuba and the Philippines gain independence from Spain.[7]

After the Spanish-American War ended, the Army tested and adopted many new weapons. Regular Army

The wreck of the U.S.S. *Maine*, after it mysteriously exploded, lies in the harbor of Havana, Cuba. While the explosion was first blamed on an attack by Spain, it was later found to have been caused by defective parts.

troops armed themselves with Springfield rifles, sturdier bayonets, and new firearms known as Colt .45 automatics.

In 1916, Congress passed the National Defense Act, allowing the government to order the National Guard into federal service for national emergencies. The new law reinforced the Militia Act of 1792, which obligated every able-bodied man between the ages of eighteen and forty-five to serve in the military, if called. In addition, the National Defense Act formally recognized for the first time the Army's components: the regular Army, the Army National Guard, and the Army Reserve for both officers and enlisted personnel.

World War I

As the United States entered the First World War, Congress passed the Selective Service Act of 1917, requiring all men

Alvin C. York
(1887–1964)

Sergeant Alvin C. York received the Medal of Honor for his courage during World War I. York assumed command of his platoon after his superiors were killed during a battle with the German Army. Charging against machine-gun fire, he killed 25 German soldiers and forced 132 other Germans to surrender.

between the ages of twenty-one and thirty to register for military service. More than 3.6 million American troops joined forces with England and France to fight Germany and its allies during World War I.[8]

Battling on the hills and in the woods of France, American soldiers learned new warfare techniques, using such newly developed equipment as airplanes, grenades, machine guns, and trench mortars. To maintain a steady supply of manpower, the Army trained soldiers before battle to provide well-trained replacements for weary troops on the battlefield. Although America and its allies won the war, there were more than 320,000 American casualties.[9]

American troops moving forward to the battle line in the Forest of Argonne, in France, during World War I.

George C. Marshall
(1880–1959)

General George C. Marshall directed the buildup of U.S. troops during World War I as the Army's chief of staff. Awarded the rank of general of the Army, he also served as secretary of state between 1947 and 1949. In 1947 he originated the European Recovery Plan, known as the Marshall Plan, to help promote economic recovery for European nations after World War II. He received the Nobel Peace Prize in 1953.

World War II

Americans rejoiced when World War I ended on November 11, 1918, hoping that another global war would never take place again. But Germany was eager to increase its power throughout the world. Under the leadership of Adolf Hitler, German forces invaded neighboring European countries during the late 1930s, setting off World War II in 1939. Italy and Japan joined forces with Germany to create the Axis powers. America remained neutral until the Japanese attacked the United States naval base at Pearl Harbor, Hawaii, on December 7, 1941. The United States immediately declared war on Japan, and Germany and Italy declared war on the United States. Soon American troops were fighting in both Europe and the Pacific, involved in the largest and most destructive war in the history of the world.

This poster urged Americans to support the war effort by buying bonds.

BUY WAR BONDS

Dwight D. Eisenhower
(1890–1969)

General Dwight D. Eisenhower was the supreme commander of Allied Expeditionary Forces in Western Europe during the defeat of Germany in World War II. He was awarded the rank of general of the Army. Eisenhower served two terms as president of the United States between 1953 and 1961.

More than 8.3 million men and women served in the United States Army during World War II, fighting in nearly every part of the world against the Axis powers.[10] American civilians at home produced new weapons and technology to help the cause of the United States and its allies—France, Great Britain, and the Soviet Union. By 1945 the Axis forces could no longer withstand the strength of the Allied powers. Soon after the collapse and surrender of German forces in Europe, the United States brought the war in the Pacific to a sudden end with the atomic bombing of Japan. After six long years of conflict, World War II ended in September 1945.

The Cold War and the Korean War

After World War II, the National Security Act of

1947 replaced the Department of War with the Department of Defense. The new law also created three divisions in the Department of Defense: the Department of the Navy, the Department of the Army, and the Department of the Air Force.

In the years following World War II, tensions developed between the United States and the Soviet Union. The United States accused the Soviet Union of trying to expand Communism all over the world, while the Soviets accused the United States of imperialism (the practice of gaining control over other countries). In addition, they clashed over the use of nuclear weapons. This period of time was known as the Cold War. Both powers built up arsenals of nuclear weapons for several decades. (The Cold War and the nuclear arms race ended with the collapse of the Soviet Union in 1991.)

During the Korean War, the United States and 15 other United Nations members sent troops to fight the North Korean forces that had invaded South Korea. Here, a member of the 19th Infantry Regiment uses his poncho to get protection from the biting wind and cold.

President Truman signs a proclamation declaring a national emergency and ordering United States troops into Korea.

In 1950, President Harry S. Truman of the United States and other members of the United Nations called Army troops into action again. American and allied troops were sent to Korea and charged with the task of defending South Korea from invasions by North Korean Communists. Although American and allied forces accomplished their mission, more than twenty-seven thousand Army troops died in the Korean War.[11]

The War in Vietnam

During the 1960s, United States Army soldiers took part in another war on foreign soil. The Southeast Asian country of Vietnam, formerly a French colony, was divided into North Vietnam and South Vietnam. The United States supported non-Communist South Vietnam against the forces of the Communist North. The United States sent advisors and equipment to the South Vietnamese. In 1964, North Vietnamese patrol boats clashed with two American destroyers, and in 1965, America sent two battalions of Marine combat troops to Vietnam. As the war continued, the United States sent more and more troops to Vietnam.

Many Americans protested the involvement of United States forces in Vietnam, especially as American casualties mounted. By 1973 about thirty-eight thousand U.S. Army soldiers had been killed in Vietnam, along with twenty thousand people from other branches of the U.S. armed forces.[12] During that year, the United States negotiated a cease-fire and withdrew its troops from the war-torn country. Two

Two U.S. soldiers on patrol in Vietnam. American soldiers faced the risks of stepping on exploding land mines and being ambushed by enemy soldiers concealed in the dense jungle.

years later, the Communists captured South Vietnam, ending the Vietnam War.

The Persian Gulf War

When Iraq invaded the small country of Kuwait in 1990, the United States military joined with the forces of more than twenty other countries to launch its largest operation since Vietnam. Sending more than five hundred thousand troops to the Persian Gulf, America prepared to attack Iraq.[13] Following six weeks of aerial bombing, the allied troops launched a ground war on February 24, 1991. The allies forced Iraq to retreat from Kuwait after only one hundred hours of fighting.

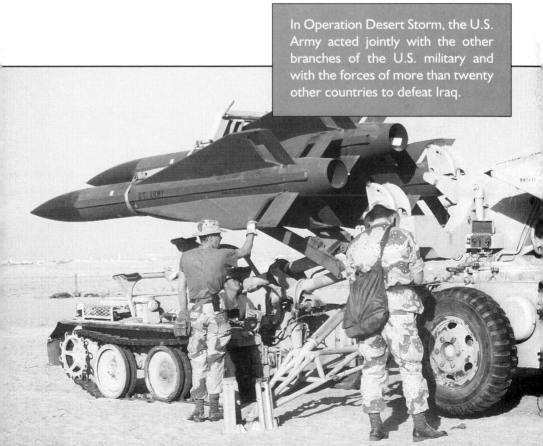

In Operation Desert Storm, the U.S. Army acted jointly with the other branches of the U.S. military and with the forces of more than twenty other countries to defeat Iraq.

H. Norman Schwarzkopf
(1934–)

General H. Norman Schwarzkopf served as the commander in chief of the U.S. Central Command during the Persian Gulf War in 1991. He directed all U.S. military operations in the Persian Gulf region. Under Schwarzkopf's leadership, U.S. and allied forces successfully defeated the Iraqi Army and liberated the country of Kuwait.

The Role of the Army

For over two centuries the United States Army has protected the interests of America and defended the rights of its citizens. Over the years the Army has developed extensive training programs, turning ordinary citizens into professional soldiers. Along with training and equipping soldiers to defend America's interests during times of war, the Army also assists other countries in their quests to preserve peace and democracy.

However, Army troops provide the United States with much more than manpower during times of war. During natural disasters and civil emergencies, units from the National Guard, Army Reserve, and regular Army help preserve peace and restore order to cities and towns across the country. Army engineers develop road systems, manage construction projects, and serve as the nation's primary source of public engineering. Thousands of U.S. troops serve as peace-keepers in countries around the globe.

The role of the United States Army has expanded greatly since the time George Washington assumed command of the nation's first soldiers. Today's troops carry out many different types of missions throughout the world to guard the nation's interests, help America fulfill its role as a world leader, and make the world a safer place to live.

**Joining
the Army**

Every year, more than 180,000 young men and women join one of three components of the United States Army: the active Army, the Army Reserve, and the Army National Guard. Another 25,000 college students become involved in the Army Reserve Officers' Training Corps (ROTC).[1]

To join any branch of the Army, you must be a citizen of the United States or have an immigrant alien card and meet certain age, health, and educational requirements. Depending on education and training, soldiers enter the Army as commissioned officers or as enlisted personnel.

Commissioned Officers

Since the Revolutionary War, the Army has depended on commissioned officers to provide leadership and direction for America's armed troops. United States Army officers are commissioned for service in the military by the president (or a leading government official acting on behalf of the president) with the approval of the United States Senate.[2]

During the American Revolution, General George Washington and other military leaders recommended the establishment of a special school for training and educating future soldiers. In 1802, Congress approved the creation of the United States Military Academy. West Point, established by the Continental Army in 1778 on the banks of the Hudson River in New York, was selected as the site of the academy.

In the beginning, West Point students, known as cadets, received training in ordnance (military supplies, such as weapons and ammunition), maintenance of artillery (weapons for discharging missiles), and engineering. Sylvanus Thayer, superintendent of the academy from 1817 to 1833, expanded the curriculum to include intense military training and civil engineering studies. He also insisted that cadets maintain high moral standards.

During the first half of the nineteenth century, the academy became the nation's leading school for science and engineering.[3] West Point graduates who studied civil engineering at the academy were responsible for the construction of many railway lines, canals, harbors, and roads throughout the nation during the 1800s.

Academy graduates, such as General Ulysses S. Grant and General Robert E. Lee, provided high standards of leadership for Army troops during battles in the nineteenth century. West Point continued to produce military leaders for the twentieth century, including General Dwight D. Eisenhower and General Douglas MacArthur, who gained fame during World War II, and General H. Norman Schwarzkopf, who led the troops in the Persian Gulf War.

Although originally established as an all-male military school, West Point began accepting female cadets for the first time in 1976. To fill the need for female officers in the Army, women make up about 15 percent of each class.[4]

During the twentieth century more and more programs in science and technology were incorporated into the curriculum at West Point. Today, West Point cadets can major in one of more than a dozen fields, ranging from the

The United States Military Academy at West Point has graduated a number of extraordinary men and women who have gone on to become great military leaders. Academy graduate General Douglas MacArthur commanded the Allied forces in the Pacific during World War II.

sciences to the humanities. Graduates receive a bachelor of science degree and a commission as a second lieutenant in the United States Army. In exchange for their free education and training, West Point cadets agree to serve a minimum of five years on active duty after graduation.[5]

To be considered for admission to the United States Military Academy, you must obtain a nomination from a member of Congress or the secretary of the Army. Only unmarried United States citizens without dependents (spouses or children) are considered for admission. Applicants must be high school graduates with good moral character and the ability to meet the academic, physical, and medical requirements of the academy.[6]

The Army also offers direct commissions for college graduates. The Army places special emphasis on obtaining officers with professional degrees who can serve as doctors, nurses, lawyers, or chaplains.

The Army Reserve Officers' Training Corps (ROTC) helps many young people complete their college education and become commissioned officers. As college students, Army ROTC cadets can earn college credits by taking ROTC classes as electives. During a four-year ROTC program, cadets receive all textbooks, uniforms, and other materials at no cost.

The Army ROTC also awards scholarships that provide money for college tuition, fees, and textbooks. Four-year scholarships are available to college freshmen. For students who are already enrolled in

A PROFESSION :

PROFESSIONAL EXPERTISE
 – TECHNICAL
 – INTELLECTUAL / THEORETICAL
 – BROAD – LIBERAL

PROFESSIONAL
RESPONSIBILITY
CLIENT –
PROFESSIONAL
RELATIONSHIP

PROFESSIONAL
CORPORATENESS
OUR PROFESSIONAL
ORGANIZATION
PERFORMS 4 KEY
FUNCTIONS

Cadets from the U.S. Military Academy attend a classroom demonstration in the department of military instruction.

college, ROTC scholarships are available for two- or three-year programs. Different levels of scholarships are awarded to applicants solely on merit. At some schools the scholarships can be worth up to $80,000 for tuition and educational fees. Scholarship winners also receive a tax-free allowance for up to ten months each year.

You can try ROTC for as long as two years (or one year with a scholarship) without any obligation to serve in the Army. If you complete the ROTC program successfully, however, you must serve full-time in the active Army or part-time in the Army National Guard or United States Army Reserve after graduation.[7]

To be eligible for an ROTC scholarship, you need to be a United States citizen with a high school diploma or an equivalent certificate. You must also meet the Army's age requirements and physical standards. Nursing students can also receive ROTC scholarships and become commissioned officers in the Army Nurse Corps after graduation.

The Army also offers opportunities for enlistees with college degrees to become commissioned Army officers. After completing basic combat and advanced training, enlistees with college degrees may apply for Officer Candidate School. If accepted, candidates are commissioned as second lieutenants after graduation.

Noncommissioned Officers and Enlisted Personnel

Each member of the United States Army has a military grade and pay rank that corresponds to his or her military title. Generally, new recruits enlist in the Army as privates, identified as pay grade E-1. The E stands for "enlisted," and the 1 denotes the lowest enlisted rank. When enlisted personnel are promoted to the rank of sergeant (E-5), they assume more leadership responsibilities and are classified as noncommissioned officers (NCOs).

In general, you may enlist in the Army at the age of seventeen with the consent of your parents. If you are eighteen years or older, your parents' consent is not required. You must also pass a physical examination. Some physical conditions such as asthma or severe flat

Private First Class Greg Vandelune fires an M-16 machine gun during Quick Reaction Training. The rugged terrain of this area, on the coast of Somalia, makes it ideal for this training.

feet may disqualify you from enlistment, but the Army can grant waivers on a case-by-case basis.[8]

Normally, you can enlist in the Army if you have a high school diploma, general equivalency diploma (GED), or college degree. The Army prefers high school graduates who have completed some courses at a postsecondary vocational/technical school.

If you have college credits or skills that are critically needed by the Army, you may be eligible to enlist at a rank higher than the usual entry rank of private.

Applicants can also sign up before high school graduation and take up to 365 days to report for duty.

Although most applicants sign up for four years in the Army, you can choose to serve two, three, four, five, or six years. The basic commitment, however, is a total of eight years, served through a combination of active and reserve duty.

New recruits receive nine weeks of basic training at "boot camp." The first two weeks of boot camp consist mainly of physical training. The recruits also learn to assemble and disassemble their rifles, and they receive training in hand-to-hand combat, hand grenades, grenade launchers, antitank missiles, and nuclear, biological, and chemical weapons. They learn to identify types of terrain by studying maps. After graduation from boot camp, recruits receive advanced individual training in their selected military occupational specialty.

Army Reserve and Army National Guard

While active-duty soldiers make full-time commitments to the United States Army, joining the United States Army Reserve or Army National Guard requires only a part-time commitment. The Army Reserve

A recruit practices with an M-16A1 rifle in the firing range during basic training.

provides the active Army with trained units and soldiers to help with national emergencies and to meet the international obligations of the United States.

Army National Guard units are state military units under the control of state governors. During peacetime, the Guard preserves order and public safety in individual states. During times of war or national emergencies, the Guard may be called into federal service by the president of the United States.

Reservists and National Guard members receive the same basic training as active-duty soldiers while attending boot camp. Then they devote one weekend each month and two weeks each year to the Army while working full-time at civilian jobs. Membership in the Army Reserve or the National Guard requires a commitment of eight years.

Joining Today's Army

If you are interested in becoming an officer in the Army, you should contact Army ROTC professors at local colleges or universities or obtain application forms from the United States Military Academy. A third option is to talk with an Army recruiter at one of the more than fifteen hundred recruiting stations throughout the country. Army recruiters are available to answer questions about Army careers and to guide applicants through the enlistment process.

At the recruiting center, applicants take a computerized screening test and learn about various enlistment options. Then applicants proceed to the

Two soldiers from the Army National Guard move a pole after tearing down their work tent in Guyana, South America. Most of the time, members of the National Guard preserve order and public safety in their own states.

military enlistment process-ing station for a physical examination and a three-hour aptitude test. The test results reveal the types of Army careers that are the best matches for an enlist-ment candidate's interests, abilities, and preferences. Army guidance counselors review educational and career options with each candidate.

Some skills have a high priority in the Army, depending on the Army's current manpower needs for certain specialties. Applicants who enlist and qualify for training in one of the Army's critical specialties may receive a substantial cash bonus. The amount depends on the length of enlistment and the availabil-ity of personnel in that specialty. Currently, eligible candidates can receive enlistment bonuses of up to $20,000 after they enlist and successfully complete their advanced training in a critical specialty. Soldiers receive the cash bonuses in addition to their regular pay and allowances.[9]

After an applicant decides on available enlistment choices, the Army draws up a contract that spells out the terms of the person's enlistment. After the enlistment contract is signed, the new recruit travels at government expense to an Army installation to begin basic training.

Private First Class Bradley learns how to replace the power supply on a computer. Many people join the Army to take advantage of the special training opportunities.

Many people join the United States Army to take advantage of specialized training and education that will prepare them for success in the civilian world when they have completed their term of enlistment. According to annual surveys, the most popular reasons for joining the United States Army are:

1. To earn money for college

2. To receive skill training

3. To serve the country

4. To improve self-confidence

5. To have a well-paying job[10]

Today's Army depends on well-trained soldiers for the protection and defense of the nation. In return for their commitment to the country, United States Army soldiers gain valuable knowledge and skills through Army training programs, educational opportunities, and challenging assignments.

Structure of the Army

The Department of the Army is one of three major branches of the Department of Defense; the other branches are the Department of the Navy and the Department of the Air Force. A fourth branch, the United States Marine Corps, is part of the Department of the Navy. The primary responsibilities of the military departments are to train and equip personnel to defend their country, to help maintain the peace, to provide humanitarian services, and to assist in disasters.

The secretary of defense is a member of the president's cabinet and reports directly to the president. The secretaries of the Army, Navy, and Air Force are appointed by the president and report to the secretary of defense.

The headquarters of the Department of the Army is in the Pentagon in Arlington, Virginia. The Army's headquarters consists of two

The Pentagon is the headquarters for all three branches of the Department of Defense: Army, Navy, and Air Force. It is located in Arlington, Virginia.

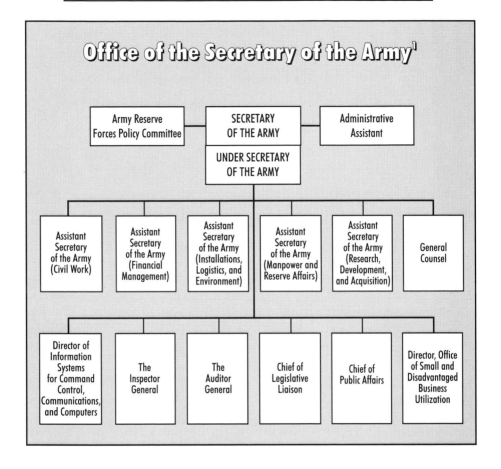

parts: the Office of the Secretary of the Army and the Army Staff.

The secretary of the Army, a civilian, is the head of the Army. As shown in the chart above, many civilian and military personnel help the secretary oversee Army operations.

The Army Staff is made up of professional military officers who advise and assist the secretary of the Army, as shown in the following chart. The chief of staff is the Army secretary's highest ranking military

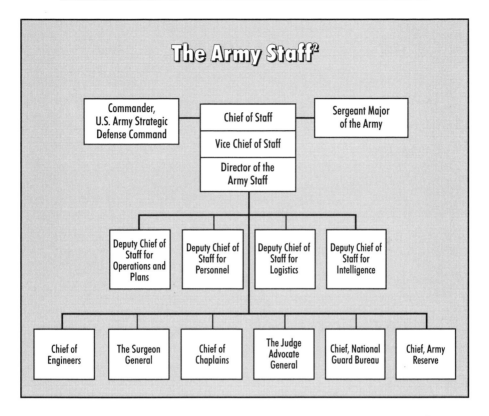

adviser. Responsible for carrying out the missions of the Army throughout the world, the chief of staff oversees the administrative, training, and supply functions of the Army and advises the president on military policies. The chief of staff has a personal staff for advice and assistance.

Size of the United States Army

The United States Army currently has approximately 488,000 soldiers on active duty, including about 220,000 enlisted personnel, 178,000 noncommissioned officers, 12,000 warrant officers, and 78,000 commissioned officers. In addition, there are 4,000 cadets at the United States Military Academy and 33,000 cadets in Army ROTC programs. About one quarter of Army troops are stationed outside of the United States, while three quarters are stationed within the continental United States.[3]

Civilians work for the Army at all levels and in all locations, freeing military personnel to carry out their missions. At the present time, the Department of the Army employs 225,000 civilians.[4]

About 39,000 commissioned officers currently serve in the Army Reserve. Reserve units include 89,000 enlisted soldiers, 76,000 noncommissioned officers, and 3,000 warrant officers, for a total Army Reserve force of 207,000.[5]

There are currently about 351,000 soldiers in National Guard units. This total includes approximately 29,000 commissioned officers, 177,000 enlisted personnel, 137,000 noncommissioned officers, and 8,000 warrant officers.[6]

Major Commands

Many of the missions of the Army are carried out through different commands. A command is a group of units and personnel that work together under one commander. Commands based in the continental United States report directly to the Army chief of staff. Outside the United States, the Army works with other branches of the armed forces in several unified commands under the direction of the Joint Chiefs of Staff. Examples of unified commands include the Eighth

United States Army in Korea and the United States Army, Europe, headquartered in Germany.

Currently, the Army depends on fifteen major commands to carry out its missions.[7]

The United States Army Materiel Command

Headquartered in Alexandria, Virginia, this command develops weapons systems, conducts research on future technologies, and maintains and distributes spare parts and equipment for soldiers and units.

Soldiers from A Company, stationed in Baumholder, Germany, arrive in Albania to provide humanitarian aid to the Kosovar Albanian refugees.

The United States Army Criminal Investigation Command (CID)

The CID provides protective services for senior Army leaders, conducts criminal investigations for the Army, has a forensic laboratory, operates a fraud unit, does narcotics investigations, and solves crimes against the Army, its soldiers, family members, and employees. The CID is headquartered at Fort Belvoir, Virginia.

The Eighth United States Army (EUSA)

This command provides forces to the commander in chief of the United Nations Command and the Republic of Korea/United States Combined Forces Command. EUSA is headquartered in Yongsan, Seoul, Korea.

The United States Army Forces Command (FORSCOM)

This command trains and deploys combat-ready troops throughout the world and is headquartered at Fort McPherson, Georgia. FORSCOM also provides military support to civil authorities, including response to natural disasters and civil emergencies.

The United States Army Intelligence and Security Command (INSCOM)

INSCOM plans and conducts intelligence, security, and information operations for military commanders. Army National Guard and Army Reserve units also support INSCOM, which is headquartered at Fort Belvoir, Virginia.

The United States Army Military District of Washington

From headquarters in Washington, D.C., this command conducts official and public events and provides support to Army operations and disaster relief efforts in the region of the capital city.

The United States Army Medical Command

This command, headquartered at Fort Sam Houston, Texas, is responsible for all health services at Army hospitals and clinics. It provides medical training and dental and veterinary services as well.

The United States Army Military Traffic Management Command

From its headquarters in Falls Church, Virginia, this command manages the transportation of troops and equipment during peace and war. It is responsible for managing ports, planning deployments, and providing traffic management services.

The United States Army Space and Missile Defense Command

Headquartered in Arlington, Virginia, this command is the Army's primary source of space and national missile defense.

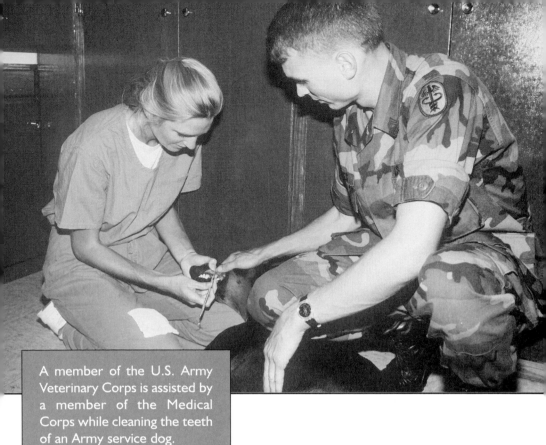

A member of the U.S. Army Veterinary Corps is assisted by a member of the Medical Corps while cleaning the teeth of an Army service dog.

The United States Army Training and Doctrine Command

This command provides training for soldiers and Army leaders and operates ten battlefield laboratories to develop and test concepts of battlefield dynamics. It is headquartered at Fort Monroe, Virginia.

The United States Army Corps of Engineers

During peace and war, this command provides engineering, construction management, and environmental services. It supports more than sixty federal agencies and responds to natural disasters as the nation's primary engineering agency.

The United States Army, Europe (USAREUR)

Headquartered in Heidelberg, Germany, USAREUR provides immediate response to NATO. It maintains a combat-ready force in Europe while monitoring armed conflicts and potential trouble areas in ninety-eight nations.

The United States Army, Pacific

This command is headquartered at Fort Shafter, Hawaii, and provides trained and combat-ready forces in the Asia-Pacific region.

The United States Army, South

Headquartered at Fort Buchanan, Puerto Rico, this command provides support to United States embassies and military groups throughout Central America, South America, and the Caribbean.

The United States Army,
Special Operations Command

Responsible for training, equipping, and deploying special operation forces throughout the world, this command includes Special Forces, Rangers, civil affairs, psychological operations, special operations aviation, and signal and support units. It is headquartered at Fort Bragg, North Carolina.

Army Branches

Today's Army is also divided into branches of service. Most branches fall into one of three categories and represent groups with similar responsibilities. Combat arms branches are directly involved in fighting, while combat support branches provide assistance to combat arms branches. Personnel in combat service support branches perform administrative functions that usually do not require any direct involvement in combat.[8]

The **Air Defense Artillery** branch defends the United States and its allies from air and missile attacks. This branch uses sophisticated weapons, such as the Patriot missile system, and operates radar and early warning systems linked to satellites in space.

United States Army Branches

Combat
Air Defense Artillery
Armor
Aviation
Corps of Engineers
Field Artillery
Infantry
Special Forces

Combat Support
Chemical Corps
Military Intelligence Corps
Military Police Corps
Signal Corps

Combat Service Support
Adjutant General Corps
Civil Affairs
Finance Corps
Medical Corps
Ordnance Corps
Quartermaster Corps
Transportation Corps

Other
Chaplain Corps
Judge Advocate General Corps

Two AH-64A Apache helicopters pass over the desert during Operation Desert Shield. The Aviation branch of the Army uses the Apache.

The **Armor** branch provides striking forces armed with tanks that can overcome an enemy with firepower and mobility. The **Aviation** branch of the Army operates such aircraft as Black Hawk and Apache helicopters.

The **Corps of Engineers** directs engineering and construction operations, ranging from building roads to constructing bridges. The **Field Artillery** branch focuses on combat power, such as rockets and missiles, and uses firepower to support the Army's ground forces.

The **Infantry** branch provides the Army with basic ground troops, while **Special Forces** conducts activities such as counterterrorism and guerrilla warfare. The **Chemical Corps** provides expertise in nuclear, biological, and chemical warfare.

The **Military Intelligence Corps** collects and assesses information about enemies and other forces that have the potential to threaten the security of the United States. The **Military Police Corps** provides security and keeps law and order in the Army community. The **Signal Corps** operates and provides information systems for the Army, such as satellite communications.

The **Adjutant General Corps** manages all military personnel activities, while the **Civil Affairs** branch establishes and maintains relationships with civilians and civil authorities in the Army's areas of operations. The **Finance Corps** takes care of financial matters for the Army, including payments to soldiers.

The **Medical Corps** provides health care services for the Army. This branch includes the Army Nurse Corps, Dental Corps, Veterinary Corps, Medical Services Corps, and Medical Specialist Corps.

The **Ordnance Corps** ensures combat power for the Army by maintaining weapons systems, ammunition, missiles, electronics, and ground mobility equipment. The **Quartermaster Corps** provides the Army with supplies, and the **Transportation Corps** furnishes vehicles and personnel to transport forces, equipment, and supplies for the Army.

An M-1A1 Abrams main battle tank arrives on a Saudi transport truck during Operation Desert Shield. Tanks are the responsibility of the Armor branch of the Army.

A military policewoman from the Army's 284th Military Police Company keeps an eye on the other members of her company as they search for unexploded mines. These soldiers are taking part in Operation Provide Comfort, a multinational effort to aid Kurdish refugees in northern Iraq and southern Turkey.

Two other combat service support branches provide the Army with special services. The **Chaplain Corps** consists of members of the clergy who offer spiritual guidance and assistance to Army personnel, while the **Judge Advocate General Corps** provides legal services for the Army.

Army Units

Units are another method of Army organization. The Army uses many different terms to describe units of soldiers. The chart that follows shows how these units are designated.

United States Army Formations[9]

Unit	Composition	Commander
Squad	8–12 soldiers	Staff Sergeant
Platoon	3 squads	Lieutenant
Company	3 platoons	Captain
Battalion	3 companies	Lieutenant Colonel
Regiment	3 battalions	Colonel
Brigade	3 battalions	Colonel
Division	3 brigades	Major General
Corps	3 divisions	Lieutenant General
Field Army	3 corps	General
Theater Army or Army group	3 armies	General

Careers, Pay, and Benefits

Before the early 1970s, thousands of young Americans were drafted into military service each year. National draft laws furnished the Army with an annual supply of new soldiers to meet the defense needs of the nation. When the draft ended in 1973, the Army had to fill its ranks with volunteer troops. To compete with civilian employers for qualified job applicants, today's Army offers many valuable benefits and career opportunities.

Enlistees can pursue careers in more than two hundred job categories, known as military occupational specialties. Many of the skills learned in these specialties can be easily transferred to civilian jobs, such as licensed practical nursing, food service, or helicopter repair.

The Army also offers attractive salaries to soldiers. Salary levels are based on pay grade and length of time in the service. Each soldier's pay increases with promotions, accumulated time in service, and annual pay raises for all federal employees. In addition to basic pay, soldiers receive allowances for such items as food, housing, and uniforms.

Commissioned Officers

As one of the world's largest employers, the United States Army offers many career opportunities for commissioned officers. Career fields for officers range from professional positions, such as doctors and lawyers, to careers with combat functions, such as aviators and artillery commanders.

As soon as officers receive their commissions, they enter one of the

A U.S. Army helicopter mechanic sets up a blade stowage bracket for a OH-58D Kiowa Warrior helicopter. The helicopter will be loaded into a cargo aircraft and sent to another Army base.

United States Army Commissioned Officer Ranks[1]

Pay Grade	Title
O-1	Second Lieutenant
O-2	First Lieutenant
O-3	Captain
O-4	Major
O-5	Lieutenant Colonel
O-6	Colonel
O-7	Brigadier General
O-8	Major General
O-9	Lieutenant General
O-10	General
O-11	General of the Army (wartime rank only)

branches of the Army to pursue their careers. Women can enter any branch or career field except infantry, armor, or Special Forces. College studies and professional training usually determine an officer's branch of service.

After officers complete their initial branch training, they receive technical instruction about their specific branch. Then they pursue their individual careers, developing leadership and professional skills through on-the-job training and Army instruction.

Each branch of the Army operates a school for training branch officers. Career officers receive additional training at one of the Army's service schools, such as the Combined Arms and Services Staff School, the United States Army Command and General Staff College, or the United States Army War College.

Promotions allow officers to advance in rank and pay. To be eligible for promotions, officers must have good evaluation reports and meet the Army's requirements for the advanced rank.

Military titles indicate the rank of an Army officer. Officers wear insignia, emblems that indicate their rank, on their uniforms. As officers advance, they assume more leadership

John J. Pershing (1860–1948)

General John J. Pershing became the most famous soldier of World War I with his successful command of American troops in France. Near the end of World War I, he was promoted to general of the Armies, the highest rank that any Army officer had attained since George Washington.

responsibilities and receive more pay for their services. Generally, commissioned officers enter the Army as second lieutenants.

An officer's basic pay is based on rank and length of service. First lieutenants with two years of service, for example, currently earn more than $2,400 per month in basic pay.[2] In addition to basic pay, officers receive allowances for food and housing. The Army also offers additional pay and allowances for special assignments, such as hazardous duty.

Officers in the Army Reserve and Army National Guard receive four days of active-duty pay for each weekend of training, based on their rank and pay grade. They also receive daily pay and allowances for their two weeks of annual training.[3]

Noncommissioned Officers and Enlisted Ranks

Before new recruits enlist in the Army, they take tests to measure their skills and abilities. Then they select an available military occupational specialty that best matches their preferences and skills. If they qualify for a specialty that is in great demand by the Army, they may receive an enlistment bonus after they complete advanced training in that specialty.

After successfully completing basic combat training, soldiers receive specialty training at military schools around the country. Skill-training programs last from eleven to forty weeks, depending on the amount of training required for a particular specialty.

The programs combine classroom instruction with hands-on training.[4]

Career fields in the Army offer many different occupations for soldiers. For example, the general engineering field offers specialties in carpentry, equipment operation, and surveying.

Army career fields include:

- Administration
- Aircraft maintenance
- Air defense artillery
- Air defense artillery maintenance
- Ammunition
- Armor
- Bands
- Chemical
- Civil affairs
- Combat engineering
- Electronic maintenance and calibration
- Electronic warfare/intercept systems
- Field artillery
- Food service
- General engineering
- Infantry
- Maintenance

- Mechanical maintenance
- Medical
- Military intelligence
- Military police
- Petroleum and water
- Psychological operations
- Public affairs
- Record information operations
- Recruitment and enlistment
- Signal operations
- Signals intelligence/electronic warfare
- Special Forces
- Supply and services
- Topographic engineering
- Transportation
- Visual information[5]

Promotions

All enlisted personnel have military titles that correspond to their ranks and pay grades. Soldiers wear insignia, emblems that indicate their rank and career field, on their uniforms. Most enlistees enter the Army as privates, designated by the pay grade of E-1. As soldiers advance in rank through promotions, they

Private Melvin Hurston of the 34th Signal Corps digs a foxhole at a new location for another Army regiment. The truck behind him is carrying a communications shelter.

assume more responsibilities and receive more pay for their services.

Enlistees who have completed some college or who have skills that are critically needed by the Army may be able to enter at a rank higher than the usual entry level of private.

After successfully completing four months of service, privates are eligible for promotion to a higher rank with more pay. Currently, privates with less than four months of service receive a basic salary of over $900 per month. With a promotion to the pay grade

United States Army Enlisted Ranks[6]

Pay Grade	Title
E-1	Private (less than four months of service)
E-2	Private
E-3	Private First Class
E-4	Specialist (ranks under Corporal)/Corporal
E-5	Sergeant
E-6	Staff Sergeant
E-7	Sergeant First Class
E-8	Master Sergeant/First Sergeant
E-9	Sergeant Major/Command Sergeant Major/ Sergeant Major of the Army

of E-2, the basic monthly pay rate increases to more than $1,000.[7]

Enlisted personnel in the Army Reserve and Army National Guard receive four days of active-duty pay for each weekend of training, based on their rank and pay grade. They also receive daily pay and allowances for their two weeks of annual training.[8]

Enlisted personnel with above-average skills and experience in a particular specialty may be eligible to apply for the warrant officer program or aviation warrant officer program. Warrant officers are appointed by the secretary of the Army to manage equipment and support activities. They are considered experts in their field.

Applicants for the warrant officer program must be between the ages of eighteen and forty-six and meet certain medical, security, and licensing standards. To qualify for aviation flight training, applicants must be under the age of twenty-nine and have at least fifteen semester hours of college credit. If selected for the program, candidates attend Warrant Officer Candidate School and receive more training in a chosen specialty.[9]

Warrant officers are ranked in three groups: warrant officers, senior warrant officers, and master warrant officers. Pay grades for warrant officers are different from the pay grades of enlisted personnel and regular officers. Currently, the basic pay for a warrant officer with more than two years of service is about $2,000 per month.[10]

Benefits and Retirement Pay

Officers and enlisted personnel on active duty in the United States Army receive a wide range of benefits. The Army also offers special benefit packages to members of the Army Reserve and National Guard.

All soldiers on active or reserve duty receive free medical and dental care. Dependents (soldiers' spouses and children) receive free outpatient care at military hospitals and clinics and pay some of the cost for inpatient medical treatment and dental care. For families

A warrant officer is responsible for equipment management and activity support. Chief Warrant Officer John Fowler, right, is inspecting a surveillance aircraft before takeoff.

who do not live near military health facilities, the military's medical insurance program pays 80 to 100 percent of the costs of medical care at civilian facilities.

Unmarried soldiers receive free housing and food at Army posts. Some Army installations provide on-post housing for soldiers with dependents. Single or married soldiers who live off the post may be entitled to receive allowances for food and housing in addition to basic pay.

Another benefit is thirty days of leave, or paid vacation, each year. Army personnel can travel free on regularly scheduled military flights to many destinations in the United States and overseas if space is available. Many Army installations also offer free services to help military families get the best prices on travel accommodations.

Large Army installations provide a wide variety of recreational facilities for soldiers and their families,

The commissary located on the U.S. Army base in Seoul, Korea. A commissary, or supermarket, has lower prices than civilian grocery stores.

such as swimming pools, golf courses, fitness centers, movie theaters, and libraries. Many of these services are available to soldiers at little or no cost.

Soldiers and their families receive special shopping privileges at the Army post exchange, known as the PX. The post exchange is like a department store with discounted prices on merchandise. Most Army installations also have commissaries, or supermarkets, with prices that are lower than civilian grocery chains.

Soldiers who wish to attend college before, during, or after their Army service can receive financial assistance for educational expenses through several Army programs. With a four-year enlistment, soldiers can earn up to $50,000 for college or vocational/technical training through the Montgomery GI Bill and the Army College Fund. After two years of service, soldiers can use these benefits for college expenses while they are on active duty or after they are discharged from the service.

Under the Montgomery GI Bill, active-duty soldiers contribute $100 per month to the program during their first twelve months of enlistment, for a total of $1,200. In return, the government contributes additional sums for the soldier's education expenses. The exact amount of the government's contribution depends on the length of the soldier's enlistment. Generally, the government contributes over $14,000 for a two-year enlistment and more than $17,000 for a four-year enlistment.[11]

The Montgomery GI Bill is available to any soldier who enters the Army except for West Point and ROTC scholarship officers. Soldiers who serve in the Army Reserve or Army National Guard on a part-time basis are eligible to receive about $9,000 for college expenses from the Montgomery GI Bill without making any personal contributions.[12]

Along with the Montgomery GI Bill, extra college funds are available to active-duty soldiers through the Army College Fund. Under this program, the Army contributes additional funds for college expenses.

The Army also provides financial assistance with tuition for voluntary off-duty educational programs. These programs must support the soldier's professional and personal development goals. Soldiers receive 75 percent of tuition costs, up to an annual benefit of $3,500.[13]

Soldiers who already have college loans may receive assistance under the Army's educational loan repayment program. A similar program is available to Army Reservists through a student loan repayment program.

After twenty years of duty, soldiers are eligible to retire from the Army and receive monthly retirement payments for the remainder of their lives. The amount of pay is based on rank, length of active service at the time of retirement, and average pay before retirement. Active-duty soldiers may retire and start receiving

Army personnel, such as this chemical engineer, may be eligible for loan repayment assistance for their college education.

retirement checks at any age as long as they have completed twenty years of service.[14]

Army Reserve soldiers are also eligible for retirement checks after age sixty if they have completed twenty years of active-duty or Army Reserve service. Retirement pay is based on a point system earned for active duty, reserve duty, and other activities.[15]

Retired soldiers enjoy many of the benefits available to active-duty and Army Reserve soldiers. After retirement, soldiers and their dependents remain eligible for military medical care, shopping privileges at post exchanges, travel on military aircraft, and recreational services at Army installations.

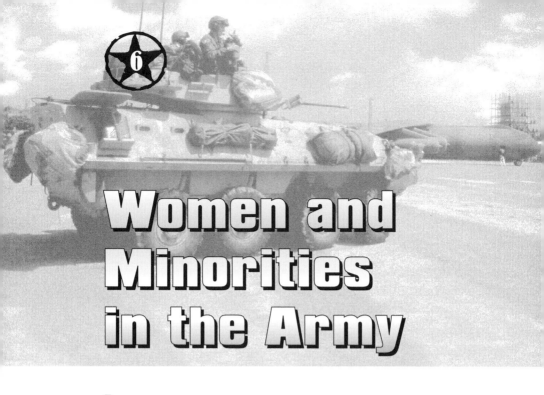

Women and Minorities in the Army

If General George Washington could see the faces of today's soldiers, he would probably be surprised to find thousands of women and members of minority groups wearing United States Army uniforms. When Washington took command of the Continental Army in 1775, white males dominated the nation's armed forces.

Today's Army offers equal opportunities to both men and women of all ethnic groups. Men and women of all races have full military status in the United States Army and serve as a strategic source of Army manpower.

Although women and minorities have played important roles of service in the United States Army since the American Revolution, they were not always regarded as official Army soldiers until midway through the twentieth century.

Past Roles of Women in the Army

During the Revolutionary War, George Washington called on women to nurse sick and dying soldiers. Nearly one hundred years later, women again served as nurses for Army troops, tending to soldiers in both Union and Confederate hospitals during the Civil War.

But these women were not considered members of the military. Although some received pay for their services from the government or the Army, many were actually employed by private organizations, such as the Red Cross.

At the end of the nineteenth century, more than fifteen hundred women volunteered to serve the Army as nurses during the Spanish-American War.[1] The tremendous number of volunteer nurses convinced the government to establish a permanent source of nurses for the Army.

In 1901, Congress established the all-female Nurse Corps as a permanent branch of the Army's medical department. Although nurses did not receive commissions as officers, they received appointments to serve in the active Army. The law also provided for reserve nurses who were willing to serve during emergencies. By 1918 the Nurse Corps was known as the Army Nurse Corps.[2]

During World War I, there were 21,480 nurses serving in the Army Nurse Corps. More than 10,000 nurses were stationed overseas, assigned to field hospitals, hospital trains, and transport ships. Recognizing the outstanding services of the Army

Captain Molly and Molly Pitcher

Before the twentieth century, women often followed their husbands to the battlefield to cook their meals, do their laundry, and otherwise care for them. During the Revolutionary War, at least two women stepped in for their wounded husbands in battle—Margaret Cochran Corbin and Mary Hays McCauly.

When British and Hessian troops attacked Fort Washington in New York in 1776, Margaret Cochran Corbin took over the job of loading and firing a cannon when her husband and the rest of the gun crew were all wounded or killed. She was badly wounded in the battle, and in 1779 she was awarded a pension by the Continental Congress. She was known for the rest of her life by the nickname "Captain Molly."

Mary Hays McCauly became known as Molly Pitcher because she carried water to thirsty soldiers at the Battle of Monmouth in 1778. When her husband William, an artilleryman, fell wounded, Molly stepped forward to take his place manning a big gun. She bravely remained at her post in the face of heavy enemy fire. Mary Hays McCauly later received a warrant as a noncommissioned officer from George Washington. (The photo at the right shows an engraving of Molly Pitcher at the Battle of Monmouth.)

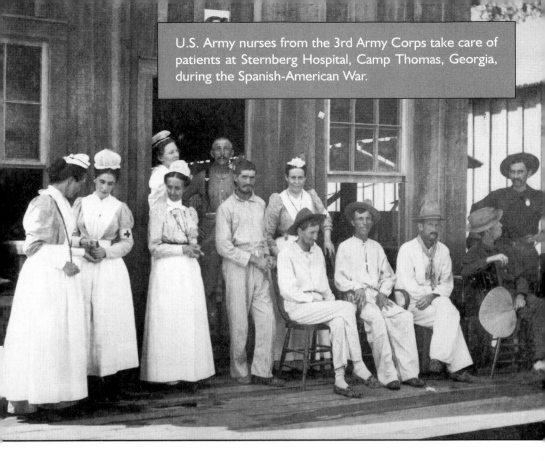

U.S. Army nurses from the 3rd Army Corps take care of patients at Sternberg Hospital, Camp Thomas, Georgia, during the Spanish-American War.

Nurse Corps during World War I, Congress passed the Army Reorganization Act in 1920. This act granted officer status to Army nurses from the ranks of second lieutenant through major, but it did not give them the same privileges, such as base pay, as regular Army officers of the same rank.[3]

The status of nurses, however, changed after the United States entered World War II. For the first time, nurses received officers' commissions, full retirement benefits, and equal pay. During the war, more than fifty-seven thousand nurses from the Army Nurse Corps served on active duty at home and overseas.[4]

During World War II, Army nurses performed their duties heroically, often in dangerous situations. In

May 1942, sixty-six Army nurses became prisoners of war of the Japanese. Lieutenant Reba Z. Whittle of the 813th Medical Air Evacuation Transport Squadron became a prisoner of the Germans in 1944 after her plane was shot down. In Italy, six Army nurses lost their lives during enemy bombing attacks in 1944.[5]

In addition to nurses, the Army needed women to serve in other fields. As more and more men were sent to the front lines to fight, the Army looked to women to help with clerical and administrative duties on the home front.

In 1942 the Women's Army Auxiliary Corps was established to ease the manpower shortage. One year later the War Department changed the name to the Women's Army Corps (WAC) and granted full military status to members of the corps. This action allowed women other than nurses to serve officially

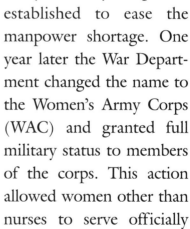

During World War II, women also helped out at home with the production of weapons and supplies. This woman is checking 1,000-pound bomb cases before they are filled with explosives and shipped to allied bases.

During World War II, Army nurses were called upon to perform their duties all over the world, often in dangerous situations. These nurses in France were also stationed in England and Egypt during their three years of service.

within the ranks of the United States Army for the first time in the Army's history.

Throughout World War II, WACs provided manpower for the Army at home and abroad. Some took over the day-to-day activities of major installations in the United States, while others helped overseas. The majority of WACs performed clerical work, although some received technical assignments, such as rigging parachutes. Before the surrender of Germany in 1945, nearly one hundred thousand WACs had served in the United States Army.[6]

More progress for women took place in 1948 when Congress established the Women's Army Corps as a permanent part of the regular Army. Another important law in 1967 removed restrictions on the careers of female military officers, allowing the same promotion procedures for both women and men. In 1970, Anna Mae Hays of the Army Nurse Corps achieved the rank of brigadier general—the first woman in history of the American military to do so.[7]

With women achieving equality in the military, the Army recognized that a separate corps for women was no longer necessary. Operations of the Women's

After the operations of the Women's Army Corps were discontinued in 1978, women moved into all branches of the Army except combat. This female soldier, servicing a CH-47 Chinook helicopter engine, is a mechanic.

Army Corps were discontinued in 1978, and women moved into all branches of the Army except combat.[8]

Members of the Army Nurse Corps continued to play vital roles in caring for wounded soldiers during the last half of the twentieth century. Nearly 5,400 Army nurses served in the Korean War. In the late 1960s and early 1970s, more than nine hundred Army Nurse Corps officers received assignments in Vietnam. Many Army nurses in Vietnam, such as First Lieutenant Sharon A. Lane, treated wounded soldiers in evacuation hospitals. Lane was wounded during an enemy rocket attack while on duty at the 312th Evacuation Hospital in Chu Lai, and she died from her injuries in June 1969. She was the only Army nurse killed as a result of enemy action during the Vietnam War.[9]

Army nurses were called into active service again during the 1990s. Over 2,200 Army nurses were deployed to the Middle East during the Persian Gulf War in 1991.[10]

Current Roles of Women

In today's Army, female soldiers receive the same pay, benefits, training, and educational opportunities as male soldiers. Current laws prohibit females from serving in military positions that require combat duties. However, women can choose from nearly two hundred occupational specialties. Taking advantage of the equal opportunities provided by the Army, women now serve in ranks ranging from private to general.

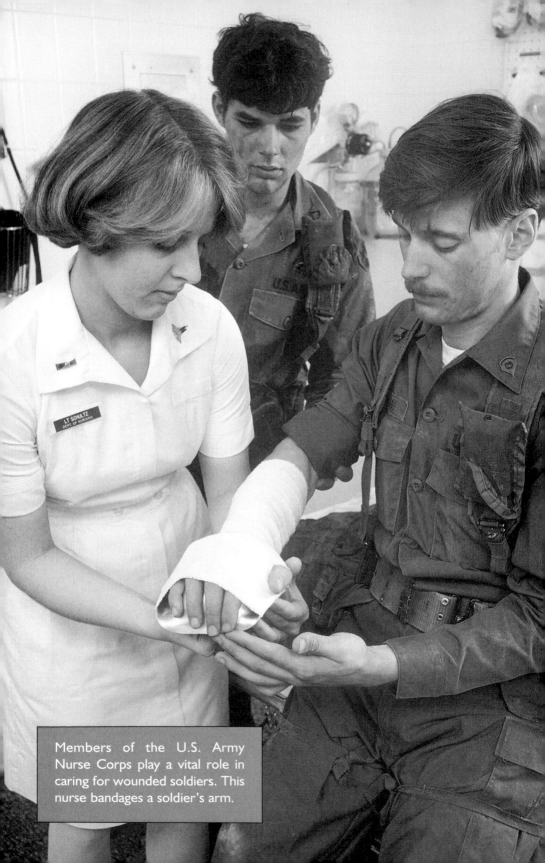

Members of the U.S. Army Nurse Corps play a vital role in caring for wounded soldiers. This nurse bandages a soldier's arm.

About 15,000 women join the United States Army each year. Today, more than 72,000 women serve on active duty in the Army, making up 15 percent, or one in seven, of the total force. About 15 percent of all women in the active Army are commissioned officers.[11]

Another 39,000 women, 3,000 of them officers, serve in the Army National Guard, making up 11 percent of the total. Women also account for 25 percent of Army Reserve personnel. Today, more than 41,000 women serve as noncommissioned officers and enlisted personnel in the United States Army Reserve.

A female drill instructor supervises recruits as they train in basic rifle marksmanship during basic training exercises.

Claudia J. Kennedy
(1948–)

Lieutenant General Claudia J. Kennedy was the first female officer in the United States Army to achieve the rank of lieutenant general. She became the Army's highest ranking woman in uniform when President William Jefferson Clinton nominated her for the three-star rank in 1997. Kennedy retired from the Army in 2000.

Another 10,000 women serve as Army Reserve officers.[12]

Past Roles of Minorities

Although many African Americans served as volunteers in the Revolutionary War and the War of 1812, they were barred from serving in the regular Army and state militias. During the Civil War, the Army officially welcomed African-American soldiers into its ranks. The Bureau of Colored Troops, established in 1863, organized and supervised units of African-American soldiers.[13]

Nearly 180,000 African Americans served in the Army during the Civil War. African-American troops made up 9 percent of the total Union Army. Although they initially served in segregated (all–African-American) supply and labor units, African-American soldiers eventually fought in more than three dozen engagements during the war.[14]

After the Civil War, United States cavalry regiments made up of African Americans fought in the Indian wars on the frontier. Soldiers in these segregated units were known as buffalo soldiers because the frontier area was the home of thousands of buffalo. Most buffalo soldiers had served in the Union Army during the Civil War as ex-slaves or free African Americans. These African-American Army units were generally commanded by white officers.[15]

In 1877, Henry Ossian Flipper, born into slavery, became the first African American to graduate from the United States Military Academy. Flipper was commissioned as a second lieutenant in the Army after his graduation. On June 30, 1882, however, following a false charge of embezzlement, he was

This soldier from the 78th Regiment of the U.S. Colored Infantry was a drummer boy during the Civil War. Nine percent of Union troops were African-American.

court-martialed and dismissed from the Army. In civilian life, Flipper held a number of private and governmental engineering positions. He was also the author of several books. In 1999, President William Jefferson Clinton granted a posthumous presidential pardon to Lieutenant Flipper, acknowledging the officer's lifetime accomplishments.[16]

About two hundred thousand African Americans served in the United States Army during World War I. Most were assigned to segregated units in France, serving under white officers.

During World War I, most African-American soldiers were assigned to segregated units in France. The troops shown are officers of the 367th Infantry, 77th Division, stationed in France.

Although some African-American soldiers participated in combat during World War I, three fourths of them worked in labor and supply units.[17]

Eighteen African Americans in the Army Nurse Corps provided nursing services during the 1918 influenza epidemic that swept through the United States. Although these nurses lived in segregated quarters, they worked in hospitals that served both African-American and white patients in Illinois and Ohio.[18]

Shortly before the United States entered World War II, Benjamin O. Davis, Sr., became the first African American in American military history to achieve the rank of brigadier general.[19]

Another first occurred in 1942 when Lieutenant Della Raney was selected as the first African-American chief nurse in the Army Nurse Corps.[20] During World War II, about five hundred African Americans served in the Army Nurse Corps. They took care of wounded soldiers at home and in Africa, England, and the southwest Pacific.[21]

Minority groups provided the United States Army with thousands of soldiers during World War II. About 900,000 African Americans, 51,000 Puerto Ricans, and 19,500 Americans Indians served as soldiers in the Army. Other minority groups, including Chinese, Japanese, Hawaiians, and Filipinos, accounted for another 51,000 soldiers.[22]

Many soldiers of Hispanic descent fought bravely during World War II. While fighting the Japanese in

Benjamin O. Davis, Sr., was the first African American to achieve the rank of brigadier general in the U.S. Army.

the Philippines, Private First Class Manuel Perez, Jr., single-handedly killed eighteen enemy soldiers and helped his entire company advance their position. Perez received the Medal of Honor for his gallant efforts.[23]

Despite many contributions to the Army, African Americans and members of other minorities served in segregated units, usually commanded by white officers. In 1948, President Harry S. Truman issued an executive order that called for "equality of treatment and opportunity for all persons in the armed services without regard to race, color, religion, or national origin."[24] For the first time in Army history, African Americans and members of other minority groups were entitled to receive equal treatment as members of the armed forces.

The new policy opened up many opportunities for the advancement of African Americans and other minorities in the Army. Margaret E. Bailey became the first African-American nurse to obtain the rank of lieutenant colonel, in 1964. Six years later, she became the first African-American Army nurse to hold the rank of colonel. In 1979, Hazel W. Johnson-Brown of the Army Nurse Corps was promoted to the rank of brigadier general, the first African-American female general officer in the Department of Defense.[25]

General Colin Powell achieved the highest rank of any African American in the history of the United States Army when he served as the chairman of the Joint Chiefs of Staff from 1989 to 1993.

Colin L. Powell
(1937–)

General Colin L. Powell achieved the highest rank of any African-American military officer in the history of the United States. Powell served as chairman of the Joint Chiefs of Staff from 1989 to 1993, the highest military position in the Department of Defense. In 2001, he was selected to serve as secretary of state by President George W. Bush.

Current Roles of Minorities

Today's Army offers equal opportunities for all minorities. Currently, about 130,000 African Americans serve on active duty in the United States Army, making up 26 percent of the total force. Hispanics and members of other minority groups account for another 15 percent of the active Army.[26]

The Army National Guard also depends on minorities for manpower. Out of 351,000 members of the Army National Guard, African Americans make up nearly 16 percent of the total force. Hispanics and other minorities make up 11 percent of the Army National Guard.[27]

Minorities make up a large portion of the Army Reserve as well. Currently, 52,000 African Americans account for more than one fourth of the total Army Reserve force, while Hispanics and members of other minority groups make up another 15 percent.[28]

The Future of the Army

For more than two centuries, the United States Army has successfully defended the nation against threats from enemies and has protected American interests. Throughout numerous wars and conflicts, America's Army has emerged as the most powerful military force in the world.

But now, in the twenty-first century, the Army faces serious challenges on a global scale—international terrorism, threats of mass destruction, and aggressive countries with civil and military unrest. Still, after two hundred years of existence, the Army's mission remains the same: to fight and win the nation's wars and to support America's foreign policies and protect its national interests.

Today's Army supports the nation's policies and interests by maintaining a presence around the globe.

By stationing American troops at strategic places throughout the world, the Army demonstrates—both to allies and to adversaries—the nation's commitment. The Army defends national interests by guarding the safety of American citizens abroad, the security of the United States and its territories, and America's economic well-being.

To protect America's interests, the Army responds to crises and disasters by supplying troops, materials, and other support to foreign countries. By directing humanitarian efforts on foreign soil, the Army helps solve immediate problems while setting the stage for addressing more long-term issues. By responding to civil emergencies and natural disasters in America's cities and towns, the Army restores order and preserves peace at home as well.

During the twenty-first century, America's Army must continue to fight and win the nation's wars, protect national interests, train soldiers, and develop leaders for tomorrow.

To continue to help make the world a safer place, the United States Army plans to improve its response time for transferring troops, equipment, machines, and supplies to trouble spots around the world at any given time. Army leaders intend to develop the means for placing brigade combat teams anywhere in the world within 96 hours, a division on the ground in 120 hours, and five divisions within 30 days.[1]

Faster deployment of troops and equipment, however, requires changes in the Army's present operations. One of the Army's plans for improving response time is the development of lighter, more fuel-efficient vehicles. The Army hopes to replace heavy tanks and armored personnel carriers with faster, lighter machines that will be easier to transport and airlift where needed.[2]

Another goal of the United States Army in the twenty-first century is to build the first information-age Army.[3] The use of information technology will allow rapid distribution of supplies and equipment, increasing efficiency and reducing deployment time.

In the near future, the Army plans to equip its units with digital information systems. Computers and other communications devices will allow commanders and troops to acquire and share information at rapid speeds. Armed with high-tech equipment on the battlefield, every soldier will be able to learn the location of other troops and their activities through continuously updated pictures transmitted by digital cameras and computers.

One of the biggest problems facing the United States Army is the social and economic pressure to reduce defense spending. The size of the Army's force has decreased by one third since 1989, and many soldiers have been transferred back to the United States from overseas duty stations. To meet the demands for a smaller force and budget, the Army is increasing the efficiency of its operations.

To meet other challenges of the twenty-first century, the Army intends to combine active and Army

The U.S. Army will continue to respond to disasters by supplying troops and other support to foreign countries. Here a U.S. military policeman patrols the streets of Port-au-Prince, Haiti, during Operation Uphold Democracy.

Reserve forces with more frequency. American soldiers will continue to work with soldiers from the armed forces of other nations to foster international cooperation. The Army will continue to fight threats of terrorism and mass destruction by conducting training sessions to help people in cities and towns learn how to deal with these potential destructive actions.[4]

To do all this, the United States Army needs to maintain a constant supply of well-trained troops to accomplish its goals and missions successfully. The people who serve in the United States Army are the most important factors in maintaining readiness and defending the nation. To succeed in future military operations, the leadership of today's Army expects soldiers to preserve the Army's core values and adopt them as their personal code of conduct and ethics. The Army's core values are:

- **Loyalty:** Bear true faith and allegiance to the United States Constitution, the Army, your unit, and other soldiers.

- **Duty:** Fulfill your obligations.

- **Respect:** Treat people as they should be treated.

- **Honor:** Live up to all the Army values.

- **Integrity:** Do what is right, legally and morally.

- **Personal courage:** Face fear, danger, or adversity (physical or moral).

- **Selfless service:** Put the welfare of the nation, the Army, and your subordinates before your own.[5]

By following these values, soldiers will enable the Army to fulfill its responsibilities at home and throughout the world. To meet the challenges of the future, the United States Army will continue to depend on well-trained soldiers who are committed to the values of duty, honor, and country.

Army Weapons and Technology

The Gatling Gun

The Gatling gun was the first rapid-firing machine gun used by American soldiers. The Army adopted the Gatling gun in 1866. Operated manually, the gun was used in the Indian wars and the Spanish-American War. The success of the Gatling led to the development of automatic machine guns for Army troops.

M109 Howitzer

The self-propelled M109 howitzer is the United States Army's standard artillery weapon. It fires a shell 155 millimeters (about 6.2 inches) in diameter. The M109

M109 howitzer

travels about 35 miles per hour and can ford streams as deep as six feet. Carrying a crew of six, the howitzer rapidly fires rounds of highly explosive ammunition. A heavy-barrel machine gun is mounted on top of the M109. The howitzer can be transported by aircraft.

M998 HMMWV

In 1982 the Army adopted the M998 High Mobility Multipurpose Wheeled Vehicle (HMMWV), popularly known as the Humvee, or Hummer. The Humvee replaced the jeep as the Army's basic utility vehicle. It is known as the workhorse of the Army's wheeled vehicles. The Humvee, which has four-wheel drive, is used for many purposes, ranging from medical evacuations to hauling troops. Weapons, including rockets, can be attached to the Humvee and towed. The Humvee has a cargo capacity of one to two tons.

High Mobility Multipurpose Wheeled Vehicle, known as the Humvee

MIM-104 Patriot Missile System

The MIM-104 Patriot Tactical Air-Defense Missile System launches missiles from a mobile transportation unit. Powered by rocket motors, the 17-foot missiles destroy targets with shrapnel (small pieces of ammunition). The system can track eight missiles to different targets at the same time. During the Persian Gulf War, the Army successfully used Patriot missiles in combat.

M-1A1 Abrams Main Battle Tank

The M-1A1 Abrams main battle tank is the Army's most advanced tank. Mounted with machine guns, the tank contains a nuclear, biological, and chemical warfare protection system. State-of-the-art armor plates provide protection for the tank crew. The tank weighs 65 tons and can travel up to 45 miles per hour.

Patriot Tactical Air-Defense Missile System

The AH-64A Apache Helicopter

The AH-64A Apache helicopter, designed for attack missions, carries laser-guided missiles that can be launched over 3.7 miles away from a target. The Apache can also be armed with aerial rockets. The steel blades of the helicopter can withstand machine-gun strikes and cut through tree branches up to two inches thick.

NBC Toolbox

Soldiers in the field identify biological and chemical substances by using a computerized database known as the NBC Toolbox. Soldiers search the system to find instructions on how to handle harmful chemicals and give medical treatment to exposed victims. The computerized system also advises soldiers about proper decontamination procedures.

M-1A1 Abrams main battle tank

Interceptor Body Armor

Today's soldiers wear Interceptor body armor for protection against shrapnel from mines, grenades, artillery fire, mortar shells, and rifle bullets. The armor weighs about 16 pounds and consists of a vest with protective inserts and detachable neck and groin guards.

Joint Service Lightweight Integrated Suit Technology Ensemble

The Joint Service Lightweight Integrated Suit Technology ensemble protects soldiers against chemical and biological agents. The ensemble includes a garment worn over the battle dress uniform and overboots worn over standard combat boots. Soldiers wear standard combat protective gloves and masks with the ensemble, which weighs almost 10 pounds.

AH-64 Apache helicopter

The Land Warrior

Future soldiers will be high-tech fighters with the Land Warrior System currently under development. The system equips individual soldiers in the field with protective clothing, computer software, and digital cameras for sending videos back to their leaders. In addition, soldiers will have night sensors, laser lights, headsets, and microphones so they can exchange information.

The Land Warrior System

Chapter Notes

Chapter 1. The Mission and Role of Today's Soldiers

1. Renita Foster, "Bombs and Bon-bons in Bosnia," *Army Link News Page*, July 23, 1998, <http://www.dtic.mil/Armylink/news/Jul1998/a19980723bombs.html> (January 22, 2000); William A. Graves, "Soldiers Deploying to Bosnia Start Intensive Training," *Army Link News Page*, March 16, 1999, <http://www.dtic.mil/Armylink/news/Mar1999/a19990316drumbosn.html> (October 28, 1999); and Linda D. Kozaryn, "KFOR's First Priority: Countermine Operations," *American Forces Information Service Page*, June 17, 1999, <http://www.defenselink.mil/news/Jun1999/n06171999_9906176.html> (January 22, 2000).

2. "Background Notes: Bosnia," *U.S. State Department Page*, August 1999, <http://www.state.gov/www/background_notes/> (January 22, 2000).

3. "The Balkans," *Soldiers*, January 1999, p. 2.

4. Linda D. Kozaryn, "NATO Approves Bosnia Troop Cut," *American Forces Information Service Page*, November 3, 1999, <http://defenselink.mil/news/Nov1999/n11031999_9911032.html> (January 22, 2000).

5. ———, "Bosnian Relief from the Home Front," *American Forces Information Service Page*, December 10, 1997, <http://defenselink.mil/news/Dec1997/n12101997_9712102.html> (January 14, 2000).

6. "Situation Report," *Soldiers*, January 2000, p. 16.

7. "Army Operations," *Soldiers*, January 2000, p. 10.

8. "Situation Report," *Soldiers*, January 2001, p. 8.

9. Ibid., p. 9.

10. *Opportunities and Options*, fourth edition (Ft. Knox, Ky.: United States Army Recruiting Command, n.d.), p. 9.

Chapter 2. History of the United States Army

1. Erna Risch, *Quartermaster Support of the Army: A History of the Corps, 1775–1939* (Washington, D.C.: U.S. Army Center of Military History, 1989), p. 13.

2. Russell F. Weigley, *History of the United States Army* (New York: The Macmillan Company, 1967), pp. 34–35.

3. Ibid., p. 115.

4. Maurice Matloff, ed., *American Military History* (Washington, D.C.: U.S. Army Center of Military History, 1969), p. 163.

5. Ibid., p. 192.

6. E. B. Long with Barbara Long, *The Civil War by Day: An Almanac, 1861–1865* (Garden City, N.J.: Doubleday & Company, 1971), pp. 710–711.

7. Arnold G. Fisch, Jr., and Robert K. Wright, Jr., *The Story of the Noncommissioned Officer Corps: The Backbone of the Army* (Washington, D.C.: U.S. Army Center of Military History, 1989), p. 10.

8. Weigley, p. 358.

9. Matloff, p. 403.

10. Weigley, pp. 439–440.

11. Matloff, p. 569.

12. Fisch and Wright, p. 130.

13. Rebecca Robbins Raines, *Getting the Message Through: A Branch History of the U.S. Army Signal Corps* (Washington, D.C.: U.S. Army Center of Military History, 1996), p. 402.

Chapter 3. Joining the Army

1. *Opportunities and Options*, fourth edition (Ft. Knox, Ky.: United States Army Recruiting Command, n.d.), p. 47.

2. Lawrence P. Crocker, *Army Officer's Guide,* 47th edition (Mechanicsburg, Pa.: Stackpole Books, 1996), p. 39.

3. Vernon Pizer, *The United States Army* (New York: Frederick A. Praeger, 1967), p. 13.

4. "Life in the Corps," *U.S. Military Academy Page*, n.d., <http://www.usma.edu/admissions> (June 13, 2001).

5. "U.S. Military Academy History," *United States Military Academy Page*, n.d., <http://www.usma.edu/PublicAffairs/history/> (December 21, 1999).

6. "Ask GoArmy a Question," *United States Army Recruiting Page*, n.d., <http://www.goArmy.com/util/goArmy.htm> (January 4, 2000).

7. *Opportunities and Options*, pp. 41–42.

8. "Ask GoArmy a Question."

9. "Money and Benefits," *United States Army Recruiting Page*, n.d., <http://www.goArmy.com/tour/money/money.htm> (December 21, 1999).

10. *Opportunities and Options*, p. 48.

Chapter 4. Structure of the Army

1. "Organization of the Department of the Army," U.S. Army Publishing Agency, November 30, 1992, <http://books.usapa.belvoir.Army.mil/cgi-bin/bookmgr/BOOKS/R10_5/FIGFIGUNIQ1#FIGFIGUNIQ1> (January 28, 2000).

2. Ibid.

3. "Situation Report," *Soldiers*, January 2001, p. 8.

4. Ibid.

5. Ibid., p. 11.

6. Ibid., p. 10.

7. "Major Commands," *Soldiers*, January 1999, pp. 22–26.

8. Lawrence P. Crocker, *Army Officer's Guide*, 47th edition (Mechanicsburg, Pa.: Stackpole Books, 1996), p. 572.

9. James M. Morris, *America's Armed Forces: A History* (Englewood Cliffs, N.J.: Prentice Hall, 1991), p. 215.

Chapter 5. Careers, Pay, and Benefits

1. "United States Army Commissioned Officer Rank Insignia," *J.W.'s Place Page*, n.d., <http://www.maye.net/militaryinsignia/comofficers/Army_officers.html> (January 20, 2000).

2. "2000 Military Pay Tables," *Armed Forces News Page*, September 9, 1999, <http://www.armedforcesnews.com/index5.html> (January 28, 2000).

3. Lawrence P. Crocker, *Army Officer's Guide*, 47th edition (Mechanicsburg, Pa.: Stackpole Books, 1996), pp. 374, 377.

4. *Opportunities and Options*, fourth edition (Ft. Knox, Ky.: United States Army Recruiting Command, n.d.), p. 32.

5. Ibid., p. 33.

6. "U.S. Army Rank Insignia (Enlisted)," *The Adjutant General Directorate Page*, n.d., <http://www.perscom.Army.mil/tagd/tioh/rank/enlisted.htm> (January 28, 2000).

7. "2000 Military Pay Tables."

8. "Keep Moving Ahead in the Army Reserve," brochure (Washington, D.C.: U.S. Government Printing Office, February 1992).

9. "Today's Warrant Officer," brochure (Washington, D.C.: U.S. Government Printing Office, June 1998).

10. "2000 Military Pay Tables."

11. *Opportunities and Options*, p. 23.

12. Ibid., p. 24.

13. Ibid., p. 25.

14. Crocker, p. 538.

15. "Keep Moving Ahead in the Army Reserve."

Chapter 6. Women and Minorities in the Army

1. "Highlights of the Army Nurse Corps," *U.S. Army Center of Military History Page*, n.d., <http://www.Army .mil/cmh-pg/anc/highlights.html> (January 19, 2000).

2. Ibid.

3. Ibid.

4. Ibid.

5. Ibid.

6. Arnold G. Fisch, Jr., and Robert K. Wright, Jr., *The Story of the Noncommissioned Officer Corps: The Backbone of the Army* (Washington, D.C.: U.S. Army Center of Military History, 1989), pp. 100–101.

7. "Highlights of the Army Nurse Corps."

8. Judith A. Bellafaire, "The Women's Army Corps: A Commemoration of World War II Service," *U.S. Army Center of Military History Page*, n.d., <http://www.Army .mil/cmh-pg/brochures/wac/wac.htm> (January 19, 2000).

9. "Highlights of the Army Nurse Corps."

10. Ibid.

11. "Situation Report," *Soldiers*, January 2001, p. 9.

12. "Situation Report," pp. 10–11.

13. Maurice Matloff, ed., *American Military History* (Washington, D.C.: U.S. Army Center of Military History, 1969), p. 229.

14. James M. Morris, *America's Armed Forces: A History* (Englewood Cliffs, N.J.: Prentice Hall, 1991), p. 112.

15. Ibid., p. 142.

16. "Lieutenant Henry Ossian Flipper, U.S. Army, 1856–1940," *U.S. Army Center of Military History Page*, n.d., <http://www.Army.mil/cmh-pg/topics/afam/flipper.htm> (January 19, 2000).

17. Morris, p. 186.

18. "Highlights of the Army Nurse Corps."

19. "Biography of Benjamin O. Davis, Sr.," *U.S. Center of Military History Page*, n.d., <http://www.Army.mil/cmh-pg/topics/afam/davis.htm> (January 20, 2000).

20. "Highlights of the Army Nurse Corps."

21. Judith A. Bellafaire, "The Army Nurse Corps in World War II," *U.S. Army Center of Military History Page*, n.d., <http://www.Army.mil/cmh-pg/books/wwii/72-14/72-14.htm> (January 19, 2000).

22. "Minority Groups in World War II," *U.S. Army Center of Military History Page*, n.d., <http://www.Army.mil/cmh-pg/documents/wwii/minst.htm> (December 21, 1999).

23. "U.S. Army Hispanic Medal of Honor Recipients," *U.S. Army Center of Military History Page*, n.d., <http://www.Army.mil/cmh-pg/topics/hisp/Hisp-MOH.htm> (July 20, 2000).

24. "Executive Order 9981," *U.S. Army Center of Military History Page*, n.d., <http://www.Army.mil/cmh-pg/reference/integrate.htm> (January 20, 2000).

25. "Highlights of the Army Nurse Corps."

26. "Situation Report," p. 8.

27. Ibid., p. 10.

28. Ibid., p. 11.

Chapter 7. The Future of the Army

1. Gerry J. Gilmore, "Army to Develop Future Force Now, Says Shinseki," *Army Link News Page*, October 13, 1999, <http://www.dtic.mil.Armylink/news/Oct1999/a19991013shinvis.html> (October 27, 1999).

2. Ibid.

3. "United States Army Posture Statement FY00: Executive Summary," *U.S. Army Page*, 2000, p. xi, <http://www.Army.mil/aps/00/execsum.pdf> (January 29, 2000).

4. Ibid., pp. viii, x.

5. "Army Values," *Soldiers*, January 1999, p. 4.

Glossary

Army Corps of Engineers—The branch of the Army that directs engineering and construction operations.

Army Reserve—A group of soldiers who serve part-time for at least eight years, helping the active Army with national emergencies and the international obligations of the United States.

artillery—Weapons for discharging missiles; or the branch of an army armed with artillery.

aviator—The operator of an aircraft.

cavalry—Originally, an Army group mounted on horseback; currently, an Army group moving in motor vehicles or helicopters.

civilian—One not on active duty in the military.

command—A group of units that work together under one commander.

commissary—A large supermarket on an Army post.

dependent—The spouse or child of a person in the military.

draft—The system of selecting people for compulsory military service.

Humvee—A High Mobility Multipurpose Wheeled Vehicle; adopted by the Army in 1982 to replace the jeep.

infantry—Ground troops.

leave—Vacation or time off.

militia—A group of citizens organized for military service.

National Guard—State military units under the control of the governor, staffed by part-time soldiers.

ordnance—Military supplies, such as weapons and ammunition.

PX (post exchange)—A department store on an Army post with discounted merchandise.

ROTC—Reserve Officers' Training Corps, a program through which college students receive financial support for their education and become commissioned officers in the Army upon graduation.

Special Forces—The branch of the Army that conducts counterterrorism and guerrilla warfare activities.

squad—A group of 8–12 soldiers.

warrant officer—An enlisted person appointed to manage equipment and supplies.

Further Reading

Cox, Clinton. *The Forgotten Heroes: The Story of the Buffalo Soldiers*. New York: Scholastic, 1993.

Green, Michael. *U.S. Army Special Operations*. Mankato, Minn.: Capstone Press, 2000.

Greenberg, Judith E. and Helen C. McKeever. *Letters from a World War II G.I.* Danbury, Conn.: Franklin Watts, 1995.

Koons, James. *U.S. Army Rangers*. Danbury, Conn.: Children's Press, 1995.

Kurtz, Henry I. *The U.S. Army*. Brookfield, Conn.: Millbrook Press, 1993.

Langellier, J. Phillip. *Bluecoats: The U.S. Army in the West, 1848–1897*. Broomall, Pa.: Chelsea House Publishers, 1999.

Stapleton, Gerard. *Air Assault Teams*. Mankato, Minn.: Capstone Press, 1995.

Internet Addresses

United States Army Web site

<www.army.mil>

United States Army Recruiting Web site

<www.goarmy.com>

United States Army ROTC Web site

Index